PONIES

First published in Great Britain in 2019
by Wayland

Editor: Victoria Brooker
Produced for Wayland by Dynamo
Written by Pat Jacobs

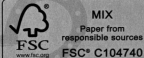

MIX
Paper from
responsible sources
FSC® C104740

FSC
www.fsc.org

HBK ISBN: 978 1 5263 1005 7
PBK ISBN: 978 1 5263 1006 4

10 9 8 7 6 5 4 3 2 1

Wayland, an imprint of
Hachette Children's Group
Part of Hodder and Stoughton
Carmelite House
50 Victoria Embankment
London EC4Y 0DZ

An Hachette UK Company
www.hachette.co.uk
www.hachettechildrens.co.uk

Printed and bound in China

Picture acknowledgements:

**All images courtesy of Getty Images iStock apart from: p6 Fell pony
Shutterstock, p16-17 tc Alamy, p18 tr Shutterstock, p24 tr Alamy**

(Key: tc-top centre, tr-top right)

CONTENTS

YOUR PONY FROM HEAD TO TAIL

Ponies have sturdy bodies, strong bones, short legs and a rounded shape. They have tough hooves and grow a thick winter coat, so they can live outdoors all year.

Withers: The bony ridge between a pony's shoulder blades.

Tail: A pony uses its tail for balance, expressing itself, and swishing away insects. The area around the top is known as the dock.

Hock: The equivalent of a human's ankle.

Fetlock: The joint above the hoof.

Frog: The triangular part of the sole of the foot that touches the ground.

Pastern: This sloping part of the foot acts as a shock absorber.

Ears: Ponies can swivel their ears and pick up sounds all around them. The sensitive area just behind the ears is the poll.

Mane: The coarse hair that grows from the crest helps a pony to swat away insects. The tuft at the front is called the forelock.

Crest: This is the top of the neck, underneath the mane.

Eyes: Because a pony's eyes are on either side of its head, it has a blind spot right infront and behind.

Muzzle: This is very sensitive. It includes the mouth, chin, lips and nose.

PONY FACTS

A pony is a small horse less than 14.2 hands tall at the highest point of the withers. A hand was originally the width of a man's hand, but it is now 10.16 cm (4 in). Ponies have stockier bodies than horses.

Cannon: The part of the leg between the hock and the fetlock.

TRADITIONAL PONY BREEDS

Ponies have adapted to live in cold, harsh environments. They have developed into tough and intelligent smaller-sized horses that are easy to keep, making them perfect family pets!

Dales ponies are known for their intelligence, stamina, strength and courage. Dales ponies are calm and kind. They have large, tough feet and strong legs with feathered fetlocks. They are sure-footed and good all-rounders.

Dartmoor ponies are reliable and hardy. They stand no more than 12.2 hands high and are usually bay, brown or black. Their size and kind temperament means they make excellent children's ponies, but they are strong enough to carry a small adult, too.

Fell ponies have heavily feathered legs and feet with strong hooves that don't often need shoes. These clever characters make good all-round family ponies, but they can be headstrong. They are sure-footed and especially suited to carriage driving.

Exmoor ponies are strong and stocky. They have adapted to cold weather and grow a waterproof winter coat with built-in insulation. These ponies are about 12 hands on average. They are good with children and adapt to all kinds of equestrian activities.

COAT COLOURS

Ponies' coats come in a variety of colours. Here are a few:

- **Bay** – rich brown body with black legs, mane and tail
- **Chestnut** – reddish-brown with no black points
- **Dun** – sandy coloured body with black legs, mane and tail
- **Roan** – an equal mix of white hairs and a pony's basic body colour, eg bay roan
- **Grey** – grey ponies have black skin with white, grey or black hair, and look grey or off-white. Pure white horses have pink skin and are very rare.

Welsh ponies are divided into sections A, B, C and D according to their size. Their personalities make them popular pets for children and they make good driving ponies, too. There's no upper height limit for section D, so many are classed as horses.

Connemara ponies are smart and willing. 'Connies' love to jump, but can turn their hooves to everything from carriage driving to dressage. These gentle, good-natured ponies are easy to keep, and at up to 14.2 hands, are great for child and adult riders.

Hackney ponies are medium-sized, high-stepping ponies. They have broad shoulders, a smooth back and a high tail. Easy to keep, they have loveable personalities. They are perfect for pulling carriages, but also make good riding ponies and companions.

Shetland ponies stand up to 10.2 hands high. They can survive harsh conditions and sparse grazing, and easily get overweight. These little ponies are intelligent and crafty – a bored Shetland will get into all kinds of mischief, so they need to be kept busy.

FIND YOUR PERFECT PONY

Buying a pony is exciting, but it's easy to fall in love with the wrong one, which can make riding less fun and unsafe. Like humans, ponies are individuals, so take time to find your perfect partner.

CHOOSE AN EXPERIENCED PONY

A young, inexperienced pony may be cheaper to buy, but it will take time to train and there's no guarantee it will be safe and reliable. It's best to choose one that is at least five years old and has been well trained so you can start riding it straight away. Ponies can be ridden into their twenties, so you will have many years of fun ahead!

SIZE IS IMPORTANT

When choosing a pony, the rider should be able to mount from the ground and their feet should not be much lower than the pony's belly. Ponies should not carry more than 20% of their bodyweight, including tack. It's tempting to buy a pony that's too large if you're still growing, but it may be difficult to control and it's a long way down if you fall.

TOP TIPS FOR PONY BUYERS

Ponies are expensive and the wrong one could be unsafe for you. Here are some tips to help.

- Take someone with you who has lots of experience with horses and ponies for independent advice.
- Choose a pony to match your skill and fitness. Your riding instructor may be able to advise on which sort of pony would suit you best.
- Handle the pony yourself and perform all the day-to-day activities, such as catching, leading, grooming and tacking up.
- Watch the pony's owner riding it before you try it out and then ask to spend some time alone with your potential new pal.
- Ask about the pony's history and look at its horse passport. If a pony has changed hands many times, it could point to a health or behavioural problem. Check that its vaccinations are up to date.
- If you are seriously interested in buying a pony, ask a vet to examine it. It can be difficult to get insurance without a pre-purchase veterinary report.

BUY OR BORROW

You can borrow a pony from a private owner or a horse charity. The upkeep costs and responsibilities will be the same, but a pony on loan from a charity will be well trained and health checked. They will be able to offer you support and advice, too!

HEALTH CHECK

- A pony should be inquisitive and alert.
- Its coat should be shiny and smooth.
- The eyes should be clear and bright.
- Its ears should be pricked, held forwards or to the side, or flicking backwards and forwards.
- The nose should be clean and the pony's breathing should be regular and steady.
- The pony should walk comfortably and evenly on all four feet.

A PLACE TO LIVE

You'll want to have everything ready to welcome your pony to its new home so the move is as easy as possible. If you've never cared for a pony before, sign up for a horse care course and take riding lessons if you're not a confident rider.

STABLING

Ponies grow thick, waterproof winter coats. Their gut produces heat as it digests fibrous food, so they have built-in central heating. They love being outdoors, but it's a good idea to put ponies in a stable at night or during bad weather. They also need to be inside if they're ill so it's easier to care for them. Stables must be well ventilated, but not draughty and make sure door bolts are pony-proof – some clever ponies learn how to open them!

PADDOCK PREPARATION

Paddock fencing must be built with horses in mind. Barbed wire is dangerous if your pony runs into the fence, and it could get its hooves caught in sheep mesh. Ponies need about 0.4 hectares (1 acre) of grazing each. Remove things that might harm your pony, such as wire, glass, bricks, stones, rubbish and poisonous plants. Fill up, or fence off, any holes. Ponies drink up to 40 litres (10 gal.) of water a day so you'll need a water tank specially designed for horses.

LIVERY

If you don't have room for a pony at home, you can keep it at a livery yard. Keeping a pony in livery will mean it has some horsey companions, and you can also get help and advice from the staff and other owners if you like. You may have access to a manege or indoor arena, too. There are different levels of livery depending on how much you are willing to pay and how much work you are prepared to do.

LIVERY CHECK

- DIY livery just includes grazing and use of a shelter or stable. The owner is responsible for all the pony's care.

- Part or assisted livery includes some help from the yard staff, such as feeding, turning out and mucking out.

- Full livery is expensive. It normally includes bedding and feed, and livery staff are responsible for all the pony's care including exercise.

- Working livery is sometimes offered by riding schools. The cost of keeping the pony is reduced because they use it for riding lessons.

UNDERSTAND YOUR PET

I'm a social creature and I don't like to live alone, so please make sure I have at least one pony pal.

BEDDING DOWN AND TACKING UP

Get some bedding to make your pony pal a soft, warm bed when it arrives. This is also the time to get all the equipment you'll need to ride and care for your new friend.

A COMFORTABLE BED

Ponies can sleep standing up, but they do like to lie down sometimes, so they need a soft bed to protect their joints. Choosing the best bedding for your stable will depend on your storage space and whether your pony is sensitive to dust, or has allergies.

Straw is cheap, but messy to store and takes up lots of space. Some ponies are allergic to it, while others like to eat it. It makes good garden compost, but it's bulky and soon makes a large muckheap.

Wood shavings are easy to store and ponies won't eat them. Droppings and wet shavings should be removed quickly to avoid a build-up of ammonia. Shavings take longer to rot down than straw and cheap brands contain lots of dust.

Shredded paper is useful for ponies that have allergies, but a large amount is needed to make a good bed. It gets blown around easily, which can make the area around the stable and muckheap untidy.

Wood pellets are eco-friendly, dust free and very absorbent. Wet patches are easy to spot and quick to remove, and it composts quickly. The pellets need soaking in water before use, which takes extra time.

Rubber matting is dust-free and easy to clean with a hose. It's expensive, but there are no extra costs. Extra bedding may be needed in a draughty stable. The stable needs good drainage and, without bedding, your pony may get dirty.

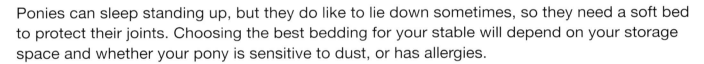

ESSENTIAL EQUIPMENT

You can save money by buying some equipment second-hand, but make sure everything is thoroughly disinfected before use. Second-hand saddles should be checked by a saddler to make sure they fit properly. Some sellers include a pony's saddle and tack so check whether you'll need to buy these. Here's a list of equipment you'll need before you bring your pony home.

EQUIPMENT CHECK ☑

- A well-fitting saddle and a saddle pad or numnah
- A bridle and bit
- A head collar
- A lead rope
- A grooming kit
- Feed and water buckets
- Mucking out equipment
- A first aid kit: bandages, cotton wool and antiseptic
- Fly repellent (if necessary)

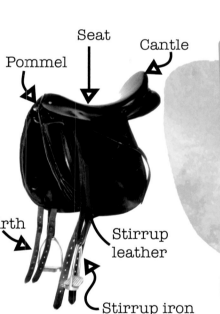

Pommel

Seat

Cantle

irth

Stirrup leather

Stirrup iron

UNDERSTAND YOUR PET

Bank up the straw at the edges of my stable, otherwise my legs may get stuck against the wall and I won't be able to get up again.

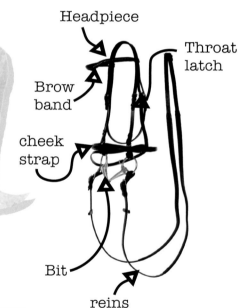

Headpiece

Throat latch

Brow band

cheek strap

Bit

reins

RIDING WEAR

A well-fitting riding hat protects you from serious injury. Make sure yours meets the current safety standards – it's best to buy from a shop with a professional hat fitter. Boots should have smooth soles and a small heel so your foot doesn't slip through the stirrups. They must be sturdy to protect your foot if a pony steps on it. Jodhpurs or riding breeches are more comfortable than jeans, for both you and your pony, and a high-visibility jacket is essential if you plan to ride on the road. Optional extras are gloves and a body protector in case you fall.

13

WELCOME HOME!

Moving to a new home can be very stressful for a pony. It has to get used to new companions, a different stable and paddock – and even the water may taste different! Try to find out as much as you can about your new friend's usual routine so you can introduce any changes slowly.

A NEW DIET

It's best to feed your pony the same food it's used to eating to start with. If possible, you should take some hay from its old home and gradually add your own to reduce the risk of colic. If you're turning your pony out, restrict it to a few hours' grazing at first and increase it slowly. Make sure it drinks enough. If not, it may not like the taste of the water so try adding a little sugar or molasses.

QUARANTINING A NEW ARRIVAL

If you have other horses or ponies, let them see the new pony from a distance at first. It's important to keep them separated for at least two weeks to avoid spreading diseases or infections. Use different food and water buckets, mucking out and grooming equipment, too. If you're caring for several horses or ponies, change your overalls and disinfect your boots when you move between them for the first few weeks. When the time comes to introduce your pony to others, turn it out with just one companion at first.

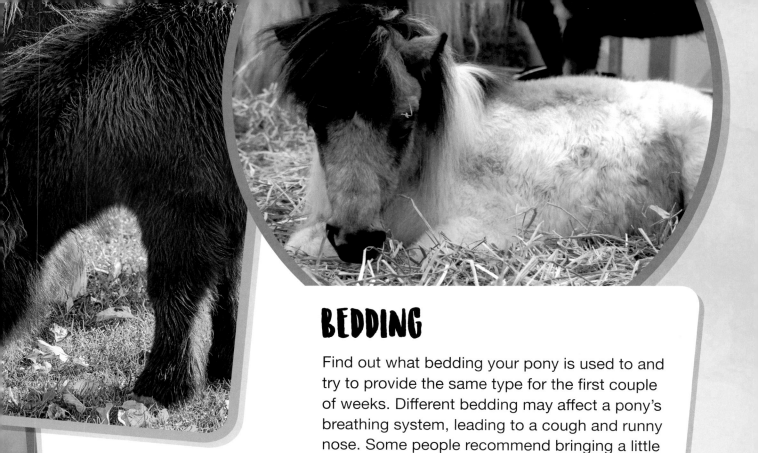

BEDDING

Find out what bedding your pony is used to and try to provide the same type for the first couple of weeks. Different bedding may affect a pony's breathing system, leading to a cough and runny nose. Some people recommend bringing a little of your pony's old bedding to its new home, so it smells familiar.

HEALTH CHECKS

Register your new pony with a vet and a farrier as soon as possible in case a problem arises. Try to avoid the stress of dental treatment, vaccinations, worming and shoeing while it gets used to its new home. It's normal for a pony's behaviour to change after moving, but if it shows signs of a cough, high temperature or loss of appetite, call your vet immediately. Once your pony has settled in, get it checked for worms.

UNDERSTAND YOUR PET

Grooming is a good way to make friends with me.

FEEDING YOUR NEW FRIEND

Ponies need to eat little and often, so it's better to give them four small meals than two large ones. They can be greedy creatures, and eating too much rich food may cause serious health problems.

WEIGHT WATCHING

A pony's natural food is grass. In the wild ponies put on weight during the summer when grass is plentiful, and lose it over winter when food is scarce. The food we give ponies today is much richer than the rough grass they would naturally eat, and because they are often stabled or rugged over winter, they don't burn off the extra fat. If your pony is overweight, give it less food over winter and don't use a rug so it burns energy to stay warm.

THE BEST DIET

Ponies have small stomachs and a very long digestive system that breaks down tough plants. They need bulky food like grass to keep their food moving through their intestines, or it can get stuck and cause colic. While grass and hay should be the main part of the diet, if a pony is exercised regularly it will need small amounts of concentrated feeds, such as cereal or sugar beet. A pony's gut is full of friendly bacteria that break down plant foods, so always change its feed gradually to give its digestive system a chance to adapt.

HOW TO FEED

Scattering food on the ground allows a pony to eat in a natural way, but it's wasteful and earth may be picked up with the feed, so it's best to put concentrated feeds in a bucket. Hay can be left in a pile on the ground and, although there will be some waste, this is safer than using a haynet because ponies can get their feet or necks caught in the net.

UNDERSTAND YOUR PET

I love treats such as carrots and apples, but cut them lengthwise and take the cores out of apples, otherwise they may get stuck in my throat.

POISONOUS PLANTS

Some common plants can be very dangerous for ponies. Learn to recognise them and remove them, or fence them off. They include ragwort, rhododendron, foxglove, yew, privet, laurel, bracken, buttercups (harmless in hay), lily of the valley, deadly nightshade, laburnum, St John's wort, sycamore and oak (leaves and acorns).

EVERYDAY CARE

Caring for a pony is hard work and you'll probably spend more time mucking out and grooming than riding. Are you up for the challenge?

PONY CARE

Daily tasks:
- Mucking out
- Grooming
- Exercising
- Feeding
- Topping up water troughs
- Picking out hooves
- Checking for signs of illness or injury

Weekly tasks:
- Removing droppings from pasture
- Checking paddocks for hazards
- Scrubbing out food and water containers

PONY CARE CALENDAR

Here's a list of jobs that are essential to keep your pony fit and healthy – and they have to be done whatever the weather! Your pony will also need regular visits from the farrier and vet for hoof trimming, reshoeing, worming, dental care and immunisations.

MUCKING OUT

Stables need cleaning at least once a day. You'll need a fork, rubber gloves, a shovel, a broom and a wheelbarrow for this job. Move droppings and wet bedding into the barrow, then sweep the floor and leave it to air for as long as possible. Then you can replace it with the clean bedding and top it up. If you can't turn the pony out, move it to one side of the stable and clean half at a time. Keep your tools away from its feet!

FOOT CARE

You should check your pony's feet every day and remove any dirt or stones using a hoof pick. Always work towards the toe so you don't damage the frog or the pony's leg if the pick slips. Ponies that are worked on roads or hard ground may need shoes to protect their hooves. Hooves should be trimmed by a farrier every ten weeks for unshod ponies, and every six weeks for shod ponies.

GROOMING

Grooming keeps your pony's coat and skin clean and healthy. It also strengthens the bond between you, and it's a chance to check for injuries. Use a curry comb in small circular movements in the opposite direction to the hair growth to loosen dirt. Flick away the dirt and loose hair with the dandy brush, then use a soft body brush to remove anything left on the surface of the coat. Clean your pony's face with a sponge or cloth and use a separate sponge or cloth for the dock area. Never share brushes and cloths between ponies because this can spread infections. Finally, untangle the tail and mane with your fingers, then brush or comb them.

YOU WILL NEED:

- A plastic or rubber curry comb
- A dandy brush
- A soft body brush
- Two damp sponges or soft cloths
- A mane comb or brush

UNDERSTAND YOUR PET

Sometimes when you're grooming me you might touch a very sensitive area and I may kick, so stand at my side, and never behind my back legs.

PONY BEHAVIOUR

Ponies communicate with one another using body language. By giving signals to other members of the herd, they are able to establish their position within the group without fighting.

YOU ARE THE BOSS

Wild ponies live in herds ruled by a stallion and an alpha mare who decide the position of all the other group members. Pet ponies also need a leader and, as ponies are large, strong animals, it's important that the leader should be their owner.

PUSHY PONIES

Ponies that are challenging your authority will crowd and push you, walk in front when you're leading them, and nip, bite or kick and step on your foot. The best way to show a pony that you're the boss is by earning its respect, which means you should be kind, but firm. Ponies can sense fear, hesitation and anger so always act calmly and confidently, and if a pony tries to move into your space, push it back.

UNDERSTAND YOUR PET

If you come straight towards me, looking me in the eye, I will probably run in the opposite direction because this means 'go away' in pony language.

EXPRESSIVE EARS

Ponies have very sensitive hearing and their ears are a clue to what they are thinking:

- Ears pricked and facing forward mean a pony is happy and interested in something.
- Ears lowered to the sides normally mean a pony is relaxed.
- Flicking ears show that a pony is listening and paying attention.
- Ears pinned flat against the neck are a warning sign that the pony is annoyed or unhappy and you should beware.

TAKING FLIGHT

Ponies are always on the look out for predators and are ready to flee if something frightens them. They have sharp senses of smell and hearing, so if they suddenly react they may have heard a noise you didn't. Pricked ears, wide eyes, flared nostrils and a raised head are a warning that a pony may bolt. If you're a nervous rider, your pony may sense this and be more jumpy. You could take lessons to gain confidence.

PONY HEALTH PROBLEMS

Ponies don't make a fuss when they're in pain, so you need to be aware of any changes that might mean they're unwell. Get to know your pony's normal heart rate, temperature and breathing rate so you'll spot if something is wrong.

LAMINITIS

Laminitis is a painful condition that affects ponies' hooves. It starts with slight lameness and can get so bad that the bone of the foot sinks through the sole and the pony has to be put to sleep. It can be caused by a past injury, stress, infection, or being worked for too long on a hard surface. Being overweight or a diet with too much sugar can cause it, too. To avoid this, be sure not to overfeed your pony and restrict grazing on sweet, new spring grass. Treatment should be given as soon as possible, so contact your vet immediately if your pony shows signs of lameness.

COLIC

Colic means stomach pain and it's common among ponies. Wild ponies graze on low-energy food throughout the day. Pet ponies often have just two feeds of rich food a day, and their guts haven't adapted to the change. Other causes can be dental problems, worms, stress or a change of diet. Signs of colic include rolling, lying down for long periods, looking at or kicking the stomach, curling the upper lip, sweating and restlessness. Call the vet if you think your pony may have colic.

STRANGLES

Strangles is a common infection of the nose and throat that is easily spread. A pony with strangles will have a high temperature, loss of appetite, yellow pus draining from the nose and abscesses may appear on the sides of the throat and head. Ponies can recover after a few weeks with good nursing.

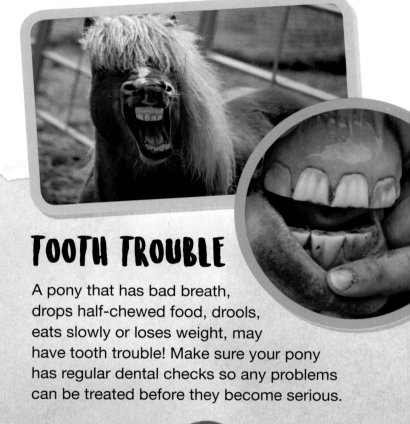

WORMING

Ponies swallow worm eggs or larvae while they graze which develop into worms in the gut. Worms lay millions of eggs that end up in the pony's droppings ready to be swallowed by another pony. Ponies get large and small redworms, roundworms, pinworms, threadworms, tapeworms, lungworms and bots. Worms are becoming resistant to wormer medicines, so have droppings tested to check the number of eggs before giving medication. Removing droppings from paddocks regularly helps reduce the eggs your pony eats.

TOOTH TROUBLE

A pony that has bad breath, drops half-chewed food, drools, eats slowly or loses weight, may have tooth trouble! Make sure your pony has regular dental checks so any problems can be treated before they become serious.

Pony manure infected with round worms.

Feed your pony puréed apple from a large syringe as a treat from time to time. It means they won't be scared of syringes when it needs worming treatment.

TRAINING

Your pony needs to learn good ground manners before you start riding it. This may take time and patience, but riding a pony that doesn't respect you is very dangerous.

GROUND MANNERS

A pony with good ground manners will stay out of your personal space, stand patiently, and allow you to clean its feet and groom it. It will also accept being haltered and led, and let you put on a bridle and saddle without moving. If a pony bites, kicks or rears, it's not safe to ride.

EARN THEIR TRUST

Wild ponies trust their leaders and follow whatever they do, so to gain your pony's respect you need to show that you're a confident leader. Ask for help from an experienced horse or pony keeper. Once your pony recognises you're the boss, don't let it get away with bad behaviour. Horses always challenge their leaders because positions in a herd change. Never train a pony by losing your temper or hurting it. Ponies are much stronger than people and it may fight back.

CATCHING YOUR PONY

Ponies can be hard to catch. If they're busy grazing, they don't always want to be interrupted. Try approaching your pony from the side and talking to it. Then offer it a treat or give it a scratch in its favourite place and walk away so it doesn't always associate being caught with something unpleasant. When you go out with a head collar, keep it hidden behind your back. Although you may be cross with your pony, you should never show this when you finally catch it.

UNDERSTAND YOUR PET

You may have to teach me something up to 60 times before I learn it, but please keep the lessons short and make them fun!

LIFTING A FOOT

If your pony is well trained it should be used to lifting its feet for cleaning and trimming. It's best to have someone to hold the pony and keep it calm while you do this. Stand to one side and stroke its back or shoulder, so it knows you're there, then run your hand down the back of the leg. When you reach the fetlock joint, lean gently against the side of the pony and lift up the foot. Never stand where you could get kicked. Remember, ponies can kick forwards and backwards.

FUN AND GAMES

HOW TO ENTERTAIN YOUR PONY

One of the main reasons for getting a pony is to work as a team and have fun together! Taking part in games is good for bonding and it stops your pony getting bored.

GYMKHANA GAMES

Here are some games you can play alone with your pony, or you can get together with friends to compete against each other. Set up your arena first and make sure you have room to turn safely.

Pole bending race – Set up five poles (or cones) in a straight line about 7 metres (23 ft) apart. The pony and rider should weave through the poles to the end of the line, then turn around and come back. The fastest time wins, but there's a five-second penalty for missing out, or touching, a pole.

Potato race – Two potatoes are placed on a barrel at the far end of the course and riders have to gallop to pick up one potato at a time then place them in a bucket back at the starting line. The winner is the rider who gets both potatoes in the bucket in the quickest time.

MAKE A PONY TOY

Rinse out a large plastic milk container and cut some holes in the side that are just a little larger than your pony's treats. Put some treats into the container and screw the lid back on. Your pony will have lots of fun playing with the container and trying to get the treats to fall out.

MAKE YOUR OWN PONY TREATS

These homemade treats are packed with all your pony's favourite foods. You can experiment with your own ingredients, but never give your pony chocolate, maple syrup, rhubarb or milk.

Ingredients:
1 grated apple (pips removed)
2 grated carrots
80 g (1/4 cup) molasses
2 tablespoons vegetable oil
125 g (1 cup) whole-wheat flour
85 g (1 cup) rolled oats
1 teaspoon salt

Preheat the oven to 180°C (350°F, gas mark 4).

Mix the apple, carrots, molasses and oil together in a large bowl, then add the flour, oats and salt. Mix together and roll into small balls. Line a baking sheet with non-stick baking paper and bake the treats for about 20 minutes until they are golden brown.

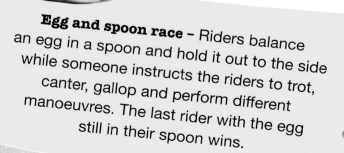

Egg and spoon race – Riders balance an egg in a spoon and hold it out to the side while someone instructs the riders to trot, canter, gallop and perform different manoeuvres. The last rider with the egg still in their spoon wins.

UNDERSTAND YOUR PET

I need to be kept busy, otherwise I'll make my own fun – and my owners don't always like that!

PONY QUIZ

By now you should know lots of things about ponies.

Test your knowledge by answering these questions:

1 **What are a pony's withers?**

a. The area around the tail

b. The bony ridge between a pony's shoulder blades

c. The joint above the hoof

2 **Where would you find a pony's frog?**

a. On its foot

b. On its back

c. On its head

3 **What is the maximum size for a pony?**

a. 12.6 hands

b. 15 hands

c. 14.2 hands

4 **What is special about a Shetland pony?**

a. It is very small

b. It has pink skin

c. It is not very intelligent

5 **Which plant is poisonous for ponies?**

a. Ragwort

b. Foxglove

c. Both of these

6 What does it mean if a pony's ears are pinned flat against its neck?

a. It is annoyed
b. It is relaxed
c. It is happy

10 What may be wrong if your pony rolls around kicking its stomach?

a. It may have worms
b. It may have strangles
c. It may have colic

7 Which body part is affected if a pony gets laminitis?

a. Tail
b. Hooves
c. Stomach

8 How often should you check your pony's feet?

a. Once a week
b. When it starts limping
c. Every day

9 Where should you stand to groom your pony or clean its feet?

a. At its side
b. Behind it
c. In front of it

QUIZ ANSWERS

1 What are a pony's withers?

b. The bony ridge between a pony's shoulder blades

2 Where would you find a pony's frog?

a. On its foot

3 What is the maximum size for a pony?

c. 14.2 hands

4 What is special about a Shetland pony?

a. It is very small

5 Which plant is poisonous for ponies?

c. Both of these

6 What does it mean if a pony's ears are pinned flat against its neck?

a. It is annoyed

7 Which body part is affected if a pony gets laminitis?

b. Hooves

8 How often should you check your pony's feet?

c. Every day

9 Where should you stand to groom your pony or clean its feet?

a. At its side

10 What may be wrong if your pony rolls around kicking its stomach?

c. It may have colic

GLOSSARY

abscess – A painful swelling on the skin, filled with pus, usually caused by an infection.

alpha – The leading animal in a group.

ammonia – A strong-smelling gas that is produced when urine reacts with bacteria in bedding or on the stable floor.

bacteria – Microscopic living things that are found everywhere. Some are dangerous and cause diseases, while others are helpful and keep animals healthy.

bit – The part of the bridle that sits in a pony's mouth.

bridle – The straps and metal fittings that are placed over a pony's head to control it.

curry comb – A tool with short teeth: plastic or rubber curry combs are used to bring dirt to the surface of a pony's coat; metal curry combs are for cleaning brushes.

dandy brush – A hard bristled-brush that should be used carefully, and only on ponies with very thick coats.

dressage – Training a pony to perform a series of movements.

equestrian – Connected with horse riding.

farrier – Someone who trims and shoes horses' hooves.

feathered – Long hair on the lower legs of some pony breeds.

fibrous food – Food that has to be chewed, such as grass and hay.

head collar – Straps that fit behind a pony's ears and around its muzzle so it can be led on a rope.

headstrong – A pony that likes to get its own way.

horse passport – A booklet that shows a pony's age, markings and breed, and lists all its owners.

immunisation – Injections that protect a pony from disease.

lameness – Limping or having trouble walking normally.

larvae – Young or newly hatched worms or insects

livery – A stable where staff look after other people's horses.

manege – An enclosed area for training horses and riders.

mare – A female horse or pony.

mucking out – removing dirty bedding from a stable.

numnah – A saddle-shaped pad, which is placed under the saddle.

pus – A thick yellow or green liquid that forms in infected flesh.

rear – To stand up on the back legs with the front legs off the ground.

saddle pad – A square or oval pad that cushions the saddle and absorbs sweat.

stallion – An adult male horse or pony.

tack – Equipment used to ride or lead a pony, such as saddles, bridles, head collars and lead ropes.

turning out – Putting a pony outside to graze.

worming – Giving a pony medicine to kill any worms or eggs in its digestive system.

INDEX